TIME OUT!

HOW TO TAKE A
MINI-RETREAT
ANY TIME
ANY PLACE

Mary Dawn Pyle

Peppertree Press
Sarasota, Florida

www.marydawnpyle.com.

Graphic design by Rebecca Barbier

For information regarding permission,
call 941-922-2662 or contact us at our website:
www.peppertreepublishing.com or write to:
the Peppertree Press, LLC.
Attention: Publisher
1269 First Street, Suite 7
Sarasota, Florida 34236

ISBN: 978-1-936051-15-1

Library of Congress Number: 2009928585

Printed in the U.S.A.

Printed May 2009

Dedication

of Gratitude

This book is dedicated to all those who need a moment of peace, and to all those who have shared their spiritual journey with me, those who have tested and challenged me, as well as those who have loved me. I am deeply indebted and thankful to many great spiritual teachers and friends. First among them are my parents, Bob and Elaine Pyle, now living as angels in my presence, who always encouraged my mind-spirit-heart connection with the God of Perfect Love.

I especially want to thank my dear friends and colleagues at The Hospice of the Florida SunCoast, St. Petersburg College, Anona United Methodist Church, First United Methodist Church of St. Petersburg, Crystal Beach Community Church, the Florida Conference of the United Methodist Church, and the faculty and staff of the University of South Florida Department of Religious Studies for the educational opportunities, friendship and support they have provided me along the way. More specifically, certain people with whom I have worked, studied and worshipped have added immeasurably to my development as a person and as a teacher. Some of those wonderful people are Dr. Jack Stephenson, Dr. Mozella Mitchell, Keith Goree, Dr. Emily Baker, Tim Arsenault, Rachelle Hutchens, Donna Daniels, Annie SantaMaria,

Dr. Jim and Judy Bradley, Dr. Susie Cashion, Dr. Wendy Coughlin, Dr. Martha Campbell, Carolyn Shoup and all the members and patients of The Hospice Pearl Team in Palm Harbor, Florida.

Along with life itself, Glenn Clark, Agnes Sanford, E. Stanley Jones, Dr. Augustine Ndeukoya, Thich Nhat Hanh, Jelaludin Rumi through the translations of Coleman Barks, Jack Cornfield, Bhante Dhammawhansha, Pema Chodron, and Eckhart Tolle have also been some of my greatest teachers, whether in person or through books and recordings.

And, most importantly, I would never have been able to survive my crazy life long enough to write this book without my family and friends. To my delightful siblings Doraine, Robert and Leon, along with their spouses and children, and to all my simply divine friends for listening, caring and encouraging me through smooth places and rough, I say thank you from the bottom of my heart. And to my patient, faithful husband, Richard, and my two beautiful daughters, Jennifer and Elizabeth, for giving me a real family, allowing me to be part of their lives, and loving me in spite of my many faults, I offer a grateful heart and much love.

To all of you, to my God the Spirit of Love, and to the Universe, I fold my hands in gratitude.

Contents

TIME OUT!

Exhale deeply and...

Chapter One

Peace Now

...inhale slowly.

Exhale deeply and inhale slowly. Imagine yourself sitting on a bed of soft, green grass on a hillside meadow looking out over a big, blue lake. The sunshine is warming your shoulders and a cool breeze freshens your face.

The smell of pine trees is in the air, and the only sound you hear is the call of a songbird in the tree above you. You have plenty of time to enjoy this place of peace.

In the time it took to read those words, your shoulders probably began to drop and your breathing slowed. Your blood pressure might have gone down a bit, and your usually busy mind knew a moment of stillness. You have experienced a mini-retreat, a brief time-out that left you feeling more relaxed and serene.

If you are like me, you are thinking how wonderful it would be to feel that way all the time. But, with all we have to do, and all there is to worry about, who can stay calm?

I confess: I am a worrier. I worry about my husband and my children, other family members, the economy, my friends, about getting older, about work that needs doing, about injustice and global conflict— well, you get the idea. I have tried for years to overcome this bothersome tendency, but I still get frazzled from time to time. Exercise, long walks, a healthy diet, a good therapist, loving supportive friends, positive thinking, prayer and meditation – all these and more, I tried. And all of them are helpful. But in the middle of a good worry session – like when I am hurrying because something is really wrong and somebody needs to fix it, and that someone must be me – I need relief and I need it now.

Not too long ago, when I was wasting a lot of time worrying about one of those things I can't control, I called a dear and very wise friend of mine who came to my house and patiently listened to me worry out loud. When I stopped complaining, she said, "I think you are in a time of transition in your life, like you are being led to use your gifts in new ways. This is exciting."

Exciting, my foot. It's stressful.

Exciting, my foot. It's stressful.

Not hearing my thoughts exactly, but recognizing the look of doubt on my face, she said, "It's natural to feel uncomfortable when we are growing and changing. There is loss and grief when we let go of what is familiar. And I hear some fear of the unknown future in your words. But this will pass if you take a time out from worry, stay open to what is happening in the moment, and just let it be."

That's easy for you to say, I continued in my silent protestation. What if I don't like what is happening?

"Try focusing on being present in the now instead of thinking constantly about the future," she added patiently, "and I think your fear will be reduced and you will be able to move forward with greater peace and serenity about the changes you are going through."

> What if I don't like what is happening?

We sipped another cup of silver needle tea and talked a while longer before it was time for her to go. As she stood to leave, I hugged her goodbye, and thanked her for listening. I promised I would do some reading on the subject of living in the now which I did. I was especially moved by the teachings I encountered in <u>A New Earth</u> by Eckhart Tolle. (You know, Oprah had a whole on-line course on the book. Of course, I had been too busy to take it at the time.) I had read and listened to tapes on this subject before, and had learned and benefitted from them, but this one, to my surprise and delight, turned out to be one of only three I have read in my life that was truly transformational. (The other two? They were the Bible and The Color Purple.) The miracles didn't start happening for me, however, until I made a decision to try practicing what I was reading about.

I began, on a daily basis, to practice pausing, being still and present in the moment. In tiny moments throughout the day, when I would catch myself worrying or hurrying or fuming, I would put the brakes on my racing mind, focus on the present, and breathe. I would slow down, look around, and notice something like the sweet smell rising from my steaming tea cup. Or the sound of an osprey calling outside my second story window. Or I would say a silent word of peaceful prayer. And then, just

And then, just for that precious moment, my worries would disappear.

for that precious moment, my worries would disappear. I felt calm, relaxed, and connected to all that is good and beautiful in nature and in life, connected to Consciousness. I could then return to my work or other activity with a clearer mind, a lighter heart, a brighter outlook, and a spirit of peace. For an even bigger change, I also began to practice being still, present, more open and compassionate with the people in my life rather than trying to fix them.

After having many of these time-out experiences that were spread out over weeks, then months, my life began to change. Emotional, mental and spiritual breakthroughs began to occur. Do you know how it feels to be in a dark room all alone not knowing if you will ever find the way out? Well, imagine you are in that room when, all of a sudden, the light goes on, and you are surrounded by pure love. Truth appears

...the light goes on, and you are surrounded by pure love

like an old friend emerging from a mist-heavy fog, and serenity spreads like the dawn's warm glow. What was once a deep, painful memory is now healed, and worries disappear (for the most part anyway – I am still a regular human being after all). For me, it was kind of like that. And these little healing miracles keep happening as long as I remember to practice my time-outs.

This book is an outgrowth and a sharing of my own efforts to establish a more peaceful way of living It is offered to you as a guidebook for retreat from the busyness and pressures of daily life for a precious moment now and then. Surely, if I, the big worrier, can take a time-out, find peace in the present moment, and go on to enjoy a blessed life, you can, too.

"Therefore I tell you, do not worry about your life, what you will eat or what you will drink... Look at the birds... And why do you worry about clothing? Consider the lilies of the field, how they grow... So do not worry about tomorrow..."

Jesus,
Matthew 6. 25-34,
The Bible, NRSV

Chapter Two

Life and How We Cope With It

Taking time out to ease the mind, body and spirit back into balance can brighten anyone's day. Some people need it more often than others, but even under the best of circumstances, we all can use a break now and then.

Stress is a part of life in this busy world. The ordinary demands of work and family can be tiring and worrisome. Just knowing that we have a deadline to meet increases the production of stress hormones that affect the body and mind, in ways both positive and negative. Driving in heavy traffic can make anyone a little crazy. In addition, some of you might be feeling intense pressures related to financial problems or conflicts in key relationships. Problems such as job loss, divorce, or major illness can produce enough stress to reduce immunity to disease, increase blood pressure, and otherwise negatively affect both physical and mental well-being in a myriad of ways. Even positive changes like starting a long-awaited new job or getting married are stress-makers.

In small doses, or when it comes only infrequently, stress may be easy to manage and release; it might even bring out the best in us in certain situations. But when stress is frequent, severe, or long-lasting, we need to reduce the tension and return to a healthy state of equilibrium before our health is damaged. Besides, you deserve some peace and serenity in your life. The question is, How do you get it?

Some popular methods of stress-reduction, such as using alcohol or prescription drugs in moderation, can help but there are risks and side-effects to consider. Counseling can be very helpful if you can find the right therapist

Exercise, yoga, prayer and meditation are some of the best antidotes for stress.

and have the insurance or other resources to cover it. Going on a real retreat to a spiritual center or relaxing spa – if you can afford the time and expense – would be delightful, but then you would have to return to your life wherein nothing has changed.

Exercise, yoga, prayer and meditation are some of the best antidotes for stress. However, many people I know believe they don't have the time, quiet space, and self-discipline required to make these practices part of their daily lives. You might have been told that you must commit an hour or more every day, and that it takes years to learn how to sit still and quiet the mind. You might even believe that you would have to move to a cabin in the woods like Thoreau, join a convent, or go to a monastery or ashram for months like Elizabeth Gilbert, if you want to find true peace. Or, worse still, that peace is only possible in the next life. The truth is, however, that with a little practice, you can learn to connect with that place of peace within you, the stillness of the present moment – anytime, anywhere – if you choose to follow a few simple steps.

Chapter Three

Any Way to Retreat Is Good

Conventional places and methods of retreat are perfectly fine when we have the time. A walk in the woods or on the beach is wonderfully refreshing. Listening to soothing music is a marvelous way to relax and unwind. Many people find solace in sitting quietly in their chosen place of worship. Others might prefer to practice retreat by sitting in silence in a quiet room at home. If you are comforted and blessed by reading a passage from a sacred text like the Bible, or another inspirational book, and sitting quietly, reflecting on what you have

19

read, that's wonderful. If you prefer to recite familiar prayers and to list or visualize the people for whom you feel concern or gratitude, that is also a beautiful way to retreat. There is no wrong way to experience peace.

Jesus often retreated from the crowds that surrounded him to spend long periods of time in solitude and communion with God. He advised his followers to go into a quiet place, shut the door and pray in private. Similarly, the Buddha taught his followers to sit in silence, quiet the mind, look deeply into a flower and feel the oneness of all things.

Some people, however, have not yet given themselves permission to retreat outside an established method, place or time of traditional worship. For others, finding a quiet place and carving out a span of quiet time can be challenging, especially for those with small children or a fast-paced work and social life. Still others find it almost impossible to quiet the mind for more than a few seconds or to sit still for more than a few minutes. The good news is that if you want the sweet rewards of retreat and you want them often, there is a way.

All time is sacred time. All places are sacred places.

The kind of retreat I am talking about requires no shrine or church, no book or prescribed methodology, no extended period of quiet time. It can be experienced wherever you are in only an instant. It can be religious or not, but experience has taught me that retreat is, by its very nature, a spiritual experience. Why? Because when you slow down to the speed of peace, you go beyond the realm of the material world. You will find the serenity you are looking for in the stillness of the present moment when the temporary no longer matters, when all that exists is the underlying reality of life itself. In that moment, you are in contact with an indefinable something Indescribably pure and beautiful, it is the essence of perfect peace. Call it what you will – God, the Infinite, the Divine, the Great I Am, Being, the Universe, a Higher Power, the Spirit of Perfect Love, Consciousness -- you can improve your conscious contact with the spiritual by opening yourself to new ways of experiencing stillness and peace. Because the Infinite is everywhere present, all around you and within you, you can touch it whenever and wherever you choose. The world is alive with it, and you are alive with it. This spiritual reality is a boundless, formless energy or power that transcends the personal, temporary self. You may benefit greatly by stretching the boundaries a little. And you can easily blend your traditional spiritual or religious practices with some of the ideas presented here to deepen and enrich your experiences of retreat.

"Be still and know that I am God."
Psalms 46.11

My hope is that this book will provide some fresh approaches to your traditional concept of retreat, enhance your spiritual practice, and hopefully, encourage and stimulate your own imagination. Your natural creativity will take you farther still on your path to peace. The practices suggested here can be used at home, at work, in the car, in the kitchen, in the bath or shower, in your own backyard, while walking the dog, or even while standing in a parking lot. They can be practiced in an elevator or on the stairs, in bed, while eating a meal, washing the dishes, or mowing the grass. When you have practiced these methods for a while, they will come so easily and naturally to you that you will be able to retreat whenever and wherever you want, whether you are alone or in a crowd.

Enjoy the journey.

Chapter Four

Practicing Presence in the Moment

The basics of <u>Time Out</u> are very simple. The practice, well, it takes practice. As you read this book and try the suggested mini-retreats, you will learn to slow down, quiet your busy mind for just a moment, and focus all your attention on the feeling of being fully alive right now. With practice, you will be able to remain in the stillness and be fully present in the moment for longer periods of time – if you choose to do so. All that is truly necessary is that you first make a decision that you want a calmer, more serene life. Then you are ready to take the second step – choosing to begin the practice. The third baby step on this transformative journey is, for just a few seconds, to slow down, notice the noisy chatter in your mind, take a deep breath, and just BE.

As I was writing this section, I couldn't help but remember the 1960s phrase made famous by an early evangelist for the wonders of LSD, Dr. Timothy Leary, who was known for saying, "Turn on. Tune in. Drop out." Don't worry. We are not about to take LSD, or any other substance for that matter. Interestingly, the steps we will apply are the exact opposite of the drug induced high. What we are doing in the mini-retreat process, might be thought of instead as tuning out the noise, tuning in to the present moment, and turning on to the power of the Spirit that is within each one of us. It is the natural process of getting high on life.

Slowing Down to the Speed of Peace

Have you ever caught yourself rushing about, making mistakes, and having to do the same thing again because it didn't go well the first time? Or maybe, at the end of a busy day, you realized that you had forgotten to do something very important. Perhaps you were so rushed you didn't enjoy the day at all. If so, I want you to know that you are not alone. I have had the same experience, and so have most all the people I know.

At first the most challenging aspect of retreat is to slow down the constant scurrying, going, and doing of our overly busy lives and to cease, or at least to turn down the volume of the constant thinking that fills our minds all day, and sometimes all night as well.

One major barrier to slowing down is the natural resistance to change. Already

I can imagine you asking, Aren't there times when we really do need to hurry like when we are taking a sick friend to the hospital, for example?

If I am honest, I have to admit that most of my hurrying is not so serious as all that, but when it is, I probably should call 911 for an ambulance instead of rushing through traffic with a sick friend in my car. Perhaps the same is true for you.

Noticing how you are living is essential if you want to make changes. As soon as you notice your mad dashing from place to place or task to task, just pause, take a mental step back, and observe your own behavior. When you are in such a hurry that your actions are less productive than they should be, you know you need to change something.

You can begin by asking yourself this basic question: Would the world really come to an end if this activity took a minute longer? You may also begin to realize that some of what you are doing might not be necessary at all, or that you could ask someone to help you. Next, you will become aware that taking a mini-retreat, a moment of time-out, will not cause any harm at all. Perhaps it will even make you more productive.

Now, if you are ready for a change, whatever you are doing at the moment – walking, talking, cleaning, computing, eating, or driving – just try to slow it down. Now begin to focus your full attention on what you are doing at this exact moment. Look, listen, touch, taste, smell, and feel what's around you and inside you. You will quickly find that the experience will be transformed from a mindless task to a precious moment.

Brushing your teeth becomes a holy act of self-care

Washing a bowl becomes a meaningful cleansing ritual, the blessing of a useful object that is usually ignored, and an opportunity for gratitude. Brushing your teeth becomes a holy act of self-care enlivening the senses of taste, touch and smell; slowing down gives you time to enjoy it. Sending an email more slowly allows you to think about what you are saying, and perhaps even to add a message of kindness. Driving to work more slowly makes you and others safer. Talking to a co-worker more slowly allows time for listening more deeply and communicating more effectively. If you are feeling stressed, slowing down while you continue your activities will instantly reduce the tension and anxiety that you are feeling.

Quieting the Busy Mind

Constant, compulsive thinking is another habit that has sometimes prevented me from experiencing the peace I needed. Whenever I find myself rehashing the same concerns again and again like a gerbil in an exercise wheel, or jumping rapidly from one thought to another,

I need to slow down my thinking process so that I can begin to think more clearly. Perhaps you can identify.

> "To recognize one's own insanity is, of course, the arising of sanity, the beginning of healing and transcendence."
> – Eckhart Tolle

Slowing down involves the mind as well as the body, but the human mind is accustomed to being constantly active. At first, when you begin the practice of focusing on the present moment, you might experience this common frustration: when you try to stop thinking, even for a few seconds, the mind will immediately fill the empty space in time with something Any thought will do. If it is pleasant memory or the happy vision of an upcoming vacation, you might want to stay with that thought for a little while. But you can't live there. Life is lived in the present.

For some of us, the first thoughts that come may be unhappy ones. Worries about what might happen tomorrow or resentments and regrets about what should not have happened yesterday often crowd out today. If this happens to you, do not be alarmed; it happens to all of us. With a little practice, you will quickly learn how to notice these thoughts and release them.

There are a variety of methods for dealing with unwelcome, unpleasant or worrying thoughts that come to mind again and again. Here are a few you can try as you begin to practice some of the mini-retreats that follow:

As you sit or stand, walk or drive, trying to enjoy a moment of peace, if an unpleasant thought pops into your head, try saying to your unhappy thought, "Hello, thought, I see you there. You can rest now because I want to feel peaceful for a while. I will take care of you later; I promise." And let the thought fly off like a passing butterfly. When the next thought comes, do the same thing And so on.

Another way of dealing with a busy mind is to hang each thought like a handkerchief on an imaginary clothesline as Howard Thurman suggested in <u>The Creative Encounter.</u> Or you may put the thought in a "God Box" or other container of your choice. If your mind goes back instantly to the same worry or to other negative thoughts, you might need to keep at it for a while. Persistence pays off.

There is yet another method you can try. Perhaps you are aware of this simple behavior modification technique that some psychologists recommend to people who can't seem to stop compulsive and/or self-defeating thinking The patient is told to wear a rubber band around his or her wrist, and every time the undesirable thought pops up, the patient is instructed to pop themselves lightly with the rubber band. It works for some people. I am not suggesting that you inflict pain on yourself, but you may try this technique if you so desire.

Usually, all that is really necessary is that you catch yourself hurrying, worrying or feeling stressed, and you are half-way there. More helpful tips and exercises will be presented in the coming chapters.

No matter what your thought habits might be, there is no need to judge or to criticize yourself for them. All human beings hurry, worry or fret at least some of the time. And judging yourself for doing so creates the opposite of the peace you want. Personally, I have found that it helps to accept my unruly thought habits as part of my normal state of being at this particular time, and to love myself anyway, just because I am a human being. Self-acceptance makes it easier to move to the next step on the journey toward serenity.

Some of you might argue that there are times when worrying is necessary, as when you've been given a serious medical diagnosis or when the economy is crashing and major financial and personal decisions must be made. In my experience, worry has been particularly counter-productive in a crisis. Instead, what I need to do when times get rough is PAUSE, OBSERVE and FOCUS – to retreat from the madness, be still, and claim a moment of peace. Challenging situations call for a calm, quiet mind that sees clearly, listens closely, feels deeply, and thinks wisely. Worry, fear, anger, guilt – these are normal human emotions which should neither be acted upon nor fought against. Fighting these feelings will only intensify them; acting impulsively on them is likely to worsen the original situation. (Unless, of course, you are fearful of an attacker, in which

PAUSE, OBSERVE and FOCUS

case it's usually best to scream and run for your life.) Your problems will be more easily resolved if you will sit still with these feelings, notice them, consider their root cause if need be, and then let these feelings go, first for a brief moment, eventually for longer periods of time. Once calm, you will be able to decide what if any action is necessary, appropriate, and morally right. If troublesome thoughts continue to plague you, a qualified professional can often help, but you can do a lot for yourself by learning to be still, observe and release the ordinary worries of life.

My mother used to say, "This too shall pass." "Let go and let God," is another oft-used phrase that carries deep meaning and immeasurable potential in times of trouble. If the God part bothers you, you might try a phrase you can more easily accept. "Let go and let life," or simply "Let it be," to quote the Beatles' song. If those don't help, you are welcome to try any phrase that does. The point is to give yourself permission to release your strangle-hold on life, to surrender for just a moment to the possibility that somehow this time of toil and trouble will pass without your controlling every little thing and every person in it, and that, no matter what problems come your way, your spirit will survive.

I invite you to use the space below to write out the thoughts that come most often into your mind when you are quiet. Look for patterns in the thoughts. And the next time you take a mini-retreat, ask your Higher Power to give you insight into what these thoughts are trying to tell you. Just writing them down may give you a fresh perspective on an old problem or help you let go of the thought altogether.

Write your thoughts here:

Chapter Five

Be the Lily in the Field

Peace is found in the present moment, when we are still, when we cease worrying about yesterday or tomorrow, when we stop struggling to make others and the world behave according to our will. To paraphrase what Jesus said, we are supposed to observe the birds and the flowers, living and growing naturally moment by moment, and be like them.

Easy to say, I hear you thinking, but not so easy to do. However, it is not as difficult as you might think. As soon you notice what you are doing and how you are thinking, you are also stopping it, if only for a split second, by becoming what Eckhart Tolle calls the observer. You have begun to watch yourself racing and spinning, and you have seen the fruitlessness of incessant movement and the constant thinking that gets you nothing but more distress. You have detached from the madness just long enough to see it for what it is. Congratulations. Now you will learn to be fully present for the many gifts of peace and joy that each moment holds in store for you.

The next step is to extend that instant of recognition for a few more seconds, and then to learn new ways of becoming fully present in the moment. The following practices are suggested as a way of holding that moment of conscious awareness and stillness for just a few seconds, then minutes, or longer. These methods can be practiced any time, anywhere. Everywhere you go, peace is there for the asking.

Focusing on your breathing is one of the easiest and best ways of learning to be present, of becoming aware of your internal state of being, and beginning to create a more peaceful life. As the tides and seasons are the rhythm of life for the Earth, breathing is the basic rhythm of your life and a key indicator of your well-being or lack thereof. When you are in a state of tension, your breathing is usually shallow and short. When you are at peace, the breath is slow and deep.

As a frothy ocean wave falls back down a steep shoreline to the sea, breathe out purposefully, deeply, noisily, fully. Then inhale slowly and naturally, as the wave returns. Repeat this process as often and for as long as necessary until you feel your shoulders drop. Your in-breath will deepen automatically, and after a few of these deep breaths, your breathing will become slower and more even. You will become aware that your belly is expanding and falling with each breath. Focus on the rising and falling of the belly. Notice that the cycle begins with the exhalation. By blowing out,... ...we are letting go of the tension. Then we begin to relax. Over time, deep breathing will become a part of every relaxation experience, and a quick and simple way to refocus your attention on what is most important – life itself.

Deep breathing involves the rising and falling of the belly, with some expansion of the chest. A healthy breathing cycle begins with a full and complete exhalation, and is followed by automatic inhalation. Whenever you feel distressed or in pain, or when you catch your thoughts or your body racing madly about, you would do well to undertake the first breathing practice as follows:

When you are involved in some activity, pause for a minute, and pay attention to your breath. Is it shallow, fast, or tight? If so, exhale deeply again and expand the belly as you inhale. Hold your breath for five seconds, then...

...blow it out fully. Hold for five seconds before you inhale again. Enjoy that moment of stillness between breaths. Without trying to control the breath, just observe the warm air moving out and the cool air moving in for the next few minutes.

Be grateful for your breath.

While you are still, remind yourself that frantic activity of mind or body is actually not more productive. Consider a better way of proceeding at a calmer, more deliberate pace.

When your breathing is slow and steady, begin to turn your attention inward. Tuning out all outside noise and activity, look with your mind's eye deep into your body to find your beating heart. After you breathe out, pause and feel your heart beating steadily in your chest. Send gratitude to your heart as you think of how it works constantly for you every day and all through the night. Breathe deeply and smile to the life-force within you.

41

Bless your life with thoughts of love and peace.
(Nhat Hanh)

This marks the end of your first mini-retreat, and the beginning of a long and wonderful journey toward a more peaceful life. Now you are ready to begin tuning in and turning on to the order, beauty and joy of life. In the following sections are some suggestions for how you can do this any time, any place.

Retreating in the Workplace

"This instant is the only time there is."

— Gerald Jampolski

Let's face it. Some jobs are much more pleasant than others. You might love your job and lose yourself in it, even take it home with you. You might be bored silly by your job, or you might actually hate the work you do, in which case you probably should be going back to school or looking for another job when the time is right. If any of these apply to you, or if you are generally content with your work, but sometimes find it stressful, taking a time-out can help.

With the time and productivity pressures often associated with work, we can easily become tense, or find ourselves so caught

43

up in the struggle to please others or to meet goals and deadlines that we lose our sense of aliveness, of conscious presence in the moment. At the same time, our perspective is altered, and we sometimes become upset about relatively insignificant issues rather than focusing on larger, more important tasks. This actually causes our performance at work to deteriorate rather than improve.

In the past, many jobs were physically unsafe, or horribly repetitive and mentally deadening. Some still are. These days, many jobs involve the constant presence and use of a computer and/or other electronic devices. When I am writing or teaching online classes, I can easily spend several hours sitting in one position before I realize how much time has passed. At that point, my body is stiff and my stomach is way past empty and feeling tight. Often my neck has been strained until a headache has set in. The only answer is to get up and move, shake out the tightness, eat something healthy, and do something else for a while.

My younger daughter Elizabeth has a similar issue in her job, but she has less freedom to get up and do something else.

The only answer is to get up and move

She has learned that the constant use of electronics can change the way the brain works, and not necessarily for the better. Consequently, she has developed a habit of turning off the computer for fifteen to twenty minutes about twice a day and doing something else like taking a walk to the water cooler, having a discussion with a co-worker, or writing on an old-fashioned pad of paper with an old-fashioned pen. Imagine that.

If you are hooked on email, an online community, or other computer-based activity, you probably need to fast from it for a period of time each day, and at least one day each week. The change of perspective will allow your brain to readjust. And you will be able to focus on your feelings and your spiritual condition instead of being constantly distracted by written and pictorial communication. Retreats just don't happen when we are "plugged in" to the electronic grid.

Likewise, if you work with numbers all day, you will probably have to deliberately engage the right side of your brain before you can experience a shift in consciousness while on the job. You could try doodling aimlessly, imagining yourself on a beautiful beach relaxing in the sunshine, or moving rhythmically to a song in your head. All these activities can be accomplished in just a moment or two, and they are powerful tools for adjusting your thinking and allowing you to move into time-out for a few minutes when you choose to do so.

It is wise to be on the lookout for symptoms of discomfort or distress, to monitor our general well-being, and notice right away any irritability in our tone of voice or body language. We should check ourselves now and then for tension in the jaw, shoulders or abdomen, and be watchful for headaches, digestive upsets, or other possible signs of stress as soon as they appear. A great deal of our happiness or unhappiness at work, and everywhere else, comes from within. So, if we are mindful, we can catch ourselves hurrying or fretting and take steps immediately to reverse the process of growing dis-ease. With a conscious decision, we can make ourselves more peaceful, effective, and enthusiastic no matter where we work or what we do.

Am I suggesting that you should be goofing off at work half the day? Absolutely not. When we are at work, we need to be at our best -- focused, calm, rational, creative, energetic -- in other words, fully present for the work at hand. Taking a break every few hours is necessary and improves productivity as well as creativity. Taking mini-retreats for a moment now and then will help relieve tension, increase your effectiveness, adjust your perspective, and add to the joy in your life. It is quick, easy and virtually invisible to others, but the results can be quickly seen in the quality of your work as well as in your mood and demeanor.

If your environment is toxic, that is abusive and/or destructive to your personhood, taking time-outs now and then probably will not be enough to protect you from harm over the long haul. It is advisable to find other work when and if you can. Such a decision should not be made hastily or lightly, however, but from a place of calm rationality. Using time-out techniques, getting in touch with your deeper feelings, analyzing your physical and financial needs, and seeking the guidance of a wise and impartial third party are advised. Mini-retreats can help you attain a calmer, more rational perspective so that you can make a wise choice.

Here are some simple time-outs you can take at work:

First, you may simply stop
what you are doing for just a
moment, close your eyes or focus your
eyes on one small and insignificant spot,
and breathe. Exhale fully, expelling any
tension. Inhale slowly and deeply. Repeat.
Deep breathing is a natural tranquilizer,
and it is often all that is needed to
find a moment of peace.

If you need to keep moving, or feel in a rush, try slowing your pace a bit. If you must continue moving quickly, begin paying attention to your breathing. Try timing your movements to your breathing and counting silently. Gradually slow your breathing as you have done before until you feel a shift in your consciousness. Remembering that a calm mind is more efficient and effective than a hurried mind, you might say to yourself, I have all the time I need to do what must be done. Slow and easy does it. Keep repeating these or similar phrases in your head until your breathing slows and your anxiety about time has been relieved.

> Notice something small – a stapler, a pen, a screwdriver, or a plant – anything will do. Look at it as if you had never seen it before, as a child might see it. Without judging it as good or bad, focus all your attention on this object for a moment. Notice that while you are focusing on this object with an open mind, your body is relaxing.

If you are feeling particularly tense, fearful or angry, physical movement is often the best way to quickly release the negative energy. You might need to take a brisk walk outside or inside the building where you work. If that is not practical, think of the way a duck shakes water off its back and do that. Shake your arms and hands, or, if no one is watching, shake your whole body. (If you

50

are concerned that others will think you are acting strangely, the restroom can be a good place to act like a duck.) Physical activity is a good way to burn excess nervous energy and to begin the relaxation process, whether you are at work, at home, or elsewhere.

Take a look around and really see what is there. Notice each item, person, or structure, each shape, texture and color. Look deeply. Without judgment, just be still with what you see.

Later, while you are calm and centered, take a visual inventory of your work area. Is your work area serene, neat and orderly? Or is it cluttered? Check your inner self. Do you feel comfortable here? If not, can you identify what is bothering you about your work space? If you can make your work space more efficient and comfortable, that's great. If not, you might consider placing in your work area an object

51

or a picture that will remind you of a peaceful, relaxing place so that every time you look at it, you will remember to take a time-out.

Be still for a moment and listen to the sounds of your workplace. Is it quiet, pleasantly noisy, or chaotic? Is there a rhythm to the sound? Just notice the sounds and be present with them for a moment. Rest while you let them be.

Later, focus on the sounds again and, this time, ask yourself how you feel with these sounds. Is your body reacting negatively or positively to the sounds? Spend a moment or two observing your feelings in response to the sounds. As you notice them, ask yourself if there are changes you can make to create a more peaceful workplace. Then do the same with the smells. Notice how you feel with these smells, and consider whether or not some fresh scent would improve your sense of serenity and well-being in your work space. Lavender is a relaxing scent many people enjoy.

Breathe deeply again, and drop your shoulders. Beginning with the top of your head and gradually moving your attention down to your toes, notice any places where tension is stored. As you become aware of the tension, let it go. Just let it flow down and out of you. See it spilling out onto the floor around you where it disappears completely. Breathe deeply one more time, and with a new sense of peace and relaxation, return your attention to your work.

While you are feeling calm, gently turn your attention inward and check your physical, emotional and spiritual condition. What feelings are present there? What is your workplace trying to tell you about your life? Listen to your inner voice speaking to you about your work environment. Be still a moment longer and tune in to the place of inner stillness that is always with you. When you return to the tasks before you, keep contact with that inner stillness as you remember what is most important – life itself and your internal peace.

As you sit or stand there in your workplace with your attention turned inward, tune out all external stimuli and focus your attention on your chest. Breathe gently and quietly for a moment until you can feel your heart beating. Pay attention to your heart and be grateful. Exhale and inhale slowly and deeply one more time. Send love to your heart, to your marvelous mind, and to your whole body. Bask in the love for a moment, and know that you can return to this feeling whenever you start to feel stressed or tired.

After you have blessed your own heart, ask your heart to send out love to all the people and/or objects around you. You may feel a relaxing warmth in your body and a deep sense of peace. When you have finished blessing everyone and everything around you, you will be able to return your attention to your work refreshed and revitalized.

Add your own ideas here:

Timing Out At Home

"When beauty is combined with stillness, it is an unbeatable combination for inner peace."

– Brian Seaward,
The Art of Calm

One of the many blessings in my life is living in a home that is usually quiet and peaceful. It is a sanctuary, a place of retreat for which I am deeply grateful. If you are fortunate enough to live in such a home, creating the retreat experience will be easy. You can, if you wish, designate a room or an area, perhaps your favorite chair, or a place on the floor where you can sit on a pillow and spend time quietly reading, praying or sitting in silence.

But home, for me and for many others, has not always been thus. I understand that one needy, unhappy or angry adult, or one normal child can dramatically alter the atmosphere in a home. Multiply that one child by three, four, or more, or add one special needs person to the mix, and home can quickly become a place of nearly constant work and severe stress with very little time or space for quiet rest. Creating mini-retreats in this environment will be more challenging, but it can be done. And, truthfully, taking time-out becomes all the more crucial to your well-being when you are so busy taking care of others.

Perhaps you are realizing at this point that your home-life is entirely too hectic. If so, it is possible that you will have to set some healthy boundaries for privacy, step outside the front door now and then, take short walks (or longer ones if you can), or ask your housemates to make some changes. But don't wait for others to change before claiming your peace. If you put the responsibility for your serenity entirely on others, chances are good that you will not have any peace at all. Warning: You might learn in this process that you are more dependent than you realized on the noises and images coming from your family, the television, computer or other devices. It might be difficult at first, but it is all the more important to separate yourself from these sounds and images for a little while each day. In time, you might choose to make significant changes in your lifestyle to increase your peace.

It is also possible to learn how to remain still on the inside while the people around you are upset or angry, but this requires a shift in consciousness, as well as practice. For most of my life, I was fearful of upsetting people. I had grown up in a home in which I was the peace-maker, the one who kept my parents from fighting, or so I thought. I felt that whenever someone was upset, it was my job to fix them, to calm them down, and to reestablish a state of peace and tranquility. Otherwise, my world might come to an end.

Thankfully, I have learned in my later years that I am not responsible for the emotional state of everyone around me and that I cannot control them anyway, no matter how hard I try. I have learned to be still and present while others are upset. For me, this is a major miracle. It has enabled me to be around and work with others I might have run from in the past. It has also enabled me to be present for others who want and need my calm support, and to model for my students a way of being present that many of them have never seen before. This shift has also greatly reduced my anxiety while giving me newfound joy, peace, and purpose. What was the secret? It was recognizing that the emotional state of another person is not about me. And that stillness and presence is the best way to help both myself and others to experience greater peace. Becoming aware was the first step. After that, the change took place over time by practicing stillness in the moment.

Sadly, for many children, women, elderly and infirm, and some healthy men as well, the home that should be their safe place is a war zone that can sometimes be deadly.

Just as in the workplace, if your home-life is emotionally toxic or physically dangerous, taking action to change your circumstances, although difficult, will be necessary. And you might need help to deal with that situation.* But, as I have previously mentioned, it is much easier to deal with big problems and make important decisions wisely when you can quiet your mind and think through your options more calmly. Taking a mental time-out will help you prepare for the next step on your journey to a better life.

Remember that you are a being of great value.

So, if you want more peace at home or in your life generally, let's put aside for now all the "reasons" we give ourselves for not taking a moment now and then to quiet our minds. Even if you are one to go all day and all evening, too, there is a way. Even if the only time you think you have to yourself is in the bed or in the bathroom, you can claim a few moments for the sake of your serenity if you choose to do so. Even if you are currently living in a toxic environment, it is possible (and necessary) to go to a quiet place within yourself for a brief period of relief. But first, you must give yourself permission to relax for a moment (or longer if possible) whenever you feel the need for a time-out. Remember that you are a being of great value. You deserve some peace and serenity in your life. You deserve a little quiet time.

Whether your home is a place where peaceful moments can be easily found if you look for them, or until the necessary changes are made, the following suggestions will be helpful for enhancing and deepening your spiritual, emotional and physical well-being:

Again, no matter what you are doing, slowing down and breathing deeply are the first resorts. Because you are always breathing, and your heart is always beating, you can practice some of the time-outs that were covered previously, especially those that are related to the breath and going inward to find and bless your heart.

Wash a dish with loving mindfulness, feeling the warm water and every movement of your hands. Caress the dish like a baby and notice its every feature. Make it your purpose to clean your mind of clutter and unhappiness as you clean the dish of bits of food. Washing and holding the dish, think these words to yourself: I am washing this dish that held my meal. As I clean this dish, I release all the tension in my arms and shoulders. As I rinse this dish, I feel my spirit washed clean. Drying this dish, I feel refreshed.

Make the bed with the same level of consciousness. Slow down enough to feel the fabric's smooth texture, its softness. Releasing thoughts of yesterday or tomorrow, or any negative energy, straighten the sheets and tuck in the blanket with your complete attention. Let your heart radiate love for the person who sleeps there as you touch the pillows.

Use the same kind of focused energy when preparing a meal, vacuuming the floor, hanging a shelf, or mowing the grass. Being fully present in the moment can turn any chore into an opportunity for joy.

Focus on your breathing while you work until your body and mind fall into a steady rhythm. Sing or hum a soothing melody, or whistle if you like, to reinforce the rhythm and the pace.

Got busy little ones at home? Teaching them to take time-out with you is one of the best things you can do for yourself and for them. Invite them to sit on the floor and make a circle with you. Place a plant, a flower, or another object of natural beauty in the floor in the middle of the circle. With enthusiasm, ask them to look closely at the object and to notice every detail about it. Let them tell you what they see. Let them touch it and smell it.

Ask them how they feel when they look at this object, and listen closely while they tell you.

Then ask them to sit very still and to breathe into it, blowing softly, then to breathe in the beauty of this bit of nature. Their imaginations will do all the work for you as you invite them to see that natural beauty within themselves. Ask them to love the beauty within themselves as they might love a little puppy or a kitten. Let them sit as long as they are able, breathing love into their own hearts, and sending it back out again to all the others in your circle. Feel free to teach them any of the other time-outs that you enjoy.

When you can, take a few minutes to sit or lie on the floor, or in a comfortable chair, and listen to some soothing music, breathe deeply and gradually relax your body from head to toe, one muscle at a time. Imagine the tension in your body flowing out and evaporating with each out-breath. Breathing in, see your body filling with a warm, golden light, the light of Perfect Love. Let it warm and comfort you for as long as you wish.

While sitting comfortably or reclining, read from an inspirational book, then close your eyes and sit with the images in your mind. Or listen to a guided meditation CD and let yourself go with the relaxing, soothing words.** By pausing the recording or remaining still after the recording has ended, you will be able to listen for the voice of your inner wisdom or your Higher Power.

Sit comfortably and light a candle. Watch the flame for a few moments, thinking of the light of the Spirit that burns within you continuously. Notice the color of the flame. Watch it dance. Let your mind absorb the light, or move into it. Become the light.

Try lying flat on your back on
the floor for a few moments practicing
breathing from the belly.
Just place your hands on your lower
belly and feel how your belly rises and
falls with each breath. As you become
more relaxed, say these words to
yourself as you breathe: Breathing
out, I release all tension from my
body. Breathing in, I feel fresh and
energized.   (Nhat Hanh)

When working with the mind and thinking
of the spirit, we often overlook or devalue the
body. But the body is precious and deserves to
be honored. One of life's greatest pleasures is
a long, warm soak in the tub. (I suggest you
lock the door to keep family members out for
a little while.) The next time you are able to
enjoy a bath, take time to touch and bless each
part of your body from the top of your head to
the tip of your toes. Say to each place you touch,

I thank you for the wondrous work you do for me each day. You are beautiful, and I bless you with gratitude, comfort, and good health.

Sit for a moment and focus on the smells in your home. Breathe with them. Notice what feelings these smells generate for you. Do they trigger a particular memory? If so, linger with that memory for a while and listen for what it has to teach you. You might want to add a soothing scent to your home environment, or to keep some fresh flowers in your home for their beauty and the sweetness of the smell.

Try eating something in silence. Look deeply into the food. Notice the sunshine, rain and earth that made it grow and remain as part of its essence. Smell it. Then feel the texture in your mouth. Close your eyes and savor the flavor. Think of nothing but the food as you eat it. What feelings does it generate for you?

When you are feeling very brave, try eating a meal without talking, or doing or thinking of anything else. Once in a while, or more often if you wish, eat an entire mean in silence like the monks do, and experience your meal in a whole new way. Focus on the sights, smells, textures and tastes of every portion and every bite of your food. You will find that when you eat more slowly you enjoy the food more fully. Your digestive process will improve and you will feel much more relaxed. Taking the meal will become a holy experience and your heart will be full of gratitude.

As much as possible, make your home a refuge from the madness of life, a sanctuary, a place of peace. If you can, designate a special place and make a regular appointment for quiet time, prayer and meditation. Uncluttering your home environment will make it more relaxing and serene. Bring healing music and a plant or flowers into your home if you can. As you learn to focus your attention on the present moment, you will be able to do so for longer periods of time. Enjoy the peace that you find within yourself. Or sit with your feelings and cradle them as you would a beloved child.

* The same thing that was said about a toxic work environment, also applies to the home, only more so. If there is verbal or emotional abuse, or physical violence, it is advisable to seek legal and/or professional help immediately to minimize the risk of serious injury or permanent damage to the body, mind and spirit.

The national hotline number to call for help with problems of domestic violence and abuse is 1-800-799SAFE (7233).

Online information is available from www.ndvh.gov as well as other sites.

** There are lots of wonderful CDs that can help you learn to relax and be still. I have produced one called "Journey into Presence." It includes three soothing mini-retreats during which you will be guided by my voice and gentle music into a state of relaxation and release. For more information about where to obtain this CD, please see my website, www. marydawnpyle.com.

Add your own ideas here:

Driving the Car

There are areas near my home where deer, wild turkey and sandhill cranes can be seen alongside an interstate highway. Safety concerns prevent me from stopping or staring, but just noticing takes my breath away. There are country roads, too, down which it is a joy to drive -- no traffic, just me and the trees, the sky, the grasses, the wildlife, and the open road. It's easy to retreat on a drive like that. Wouldn't it be wonderful if all driving was that pleasant?

Although many big-city-dwellers get around on public transit or on foot, during which time mini-retreats are relatively easy (See the next section on walking retreats.), many of us spend a lot of time driving from place to place in our own cars. We drive back and forth to work, to the grocery store, the bank, to the drug store, the dry cleaners, to the mall, to meetings, and so on and on. Oftentimes, we are operating on a tight schedule, and driving in a hurry to get to our next destination. If we are not mindful, we may become agitated or even angry, which is not only unpleasant but also unsafe. Driving in heavy traffic or with active children in the car tends to generate extra stress hormones in our body, which affect the mind, which in turn compounds the effect of stress on our body. It becomes a vicious cycle, but it can be broken. Here's how:

If you are feeling hurried while driving, first and most importantly, slow down. Take a few deep breaths and tell yourself that you are right where you are supposed to be right now. As Thich Nhat Hanh says, "Breathing in, I know I have arrived. Breathing out, I know I have arrived."

Getting somewhere else might be the practical goal, but this goal should not be our focus because the fulfillment of that goal is in the future. Instead, we should give all our attention to every movement and every decision we are making in the present moment as we drive. Driving provides a wonderful opportunity to practice presence in the moment, to breathe deeply and to quiet the mind. Remember the breathing work you have done before and use it to help you slow down and de-stress.

During a time of high stress in my own life, I found that my breathing had become shallow and short. I was driving home from work on a busy interstate highway when I realized that I was extremely tense, almost panicky. I tried to slow and deepen my breathing but it didn't work very well. What helped me most was to think this way as I drove:

I am in my car. I am driving this car on this road. I see the car in front of me. I am passing a gas station. I am in the right hand lane. I am slowing down now, preparing to turn right. I am turning right. I am straightening the wheel.

And so on like that. After a few moments of driving with this kind of mindfulness on the present moment, I began to relax and to breathe more slowly and deeply. My whole body functioned better and my mind was at ease. You can use this technique anytime you feel stressed while driving your car.

When little ones are talking, giggling, and playing in their buckled-up seats, their happy sounds can be pleasant. If so, you may relax and enjoy them. If you are in traffic, even these innocent noises might be a distraction, but they and you are safe. You are still free to focus on your driving, moment by moment, which will help you remain calm. However, when children get too loud or rough with each other, or if they get out of their seat-belts, it is oftentimes necessary to pull over and stop the car until peace and safety can be restored.

Remaining calm and present yourself, although challenging, is the best way to respond to rowdy children (or adults) in most cases. In addition, children can be taught at home to practice time-out with you. In fact, they are usually better than most adults at learning quickly how to focus and breathe to calm themselves. If they have been previously trained, you will be able to take a time-out together in the car.

Ask the children to stop and breathe with you. Making it a pleasant time rather than a punishment, ask them to find something beautiful on which to focus their attention. As one of the children locates a bird, a tree, a flower, a person, or even a house, take a group time-out for just a moment and breathe in the beauty. Remind the children (and yourself) that their spirit is a perfect flower growing and blooming within each of them. This flower must be nourished with care and love in order to thrive. Breathing in and out while we focus on the good is one of the best ways to nourish the spirit and restore calm. When everyone is back in their seats and buckled up, driving may resume – until the next time.

Driving alone provides a great opportunity to listen to soothing music or an inspirational CD. It can also be a great time for talking with your Higher Power or your Inner Wisdom. A good friend of mine, who was for many years a Catholic priest, told me that he likes to talk with God while driving his car. He "visualizes" a Holy Presence in the seat beside him and feels that Presence as loving and accepting In the cocoon of his car, while driving from one meeting to another, he is able to commune with his God, share his innermost feelings, receive guidance and inspiration, and regain his inner peace. I like to do the same, sometimes reaching out to touch the Presence beside me, holding hands as it were, with the Divine.

Next time you are out and about in your car, try "retreating" while you are waiting at a red light. Rather than fretting or fuming about the time you are losing, take the time to focus on the present moment. Breathe deeply and think or say out loud as I sometimes do, "This is a good time to relax for a moment. I am sitting comfortably in my car. All is well in this moment. I have arrived in this moment. I am exactly where I am supposed to be right now and I am at peace."

Go ahead and have that conversation with Spirit that you've been putting off for a better time. Sit still and breathe. And listen for the "still, small voice" of wisdom as it speaks to you.

Talk to yourself in soothing, loving tones. Or sing 'til your heart's content. Your car is a safe place to speak or sing whatever you want as loudly as you wish!

Add your own ideas here:

Getting Outdoors

When I was a little girl, I would frequently slip outside after dinner and go to the middle of the back yard where there were no trees overhead. I would lie down flat on my back, look up at the stars in awe, and talk to God. Sometimes God would talk back. These days, I am less likely to lie down on the ground, but I still go outside and look up. Noticing the immensity of the universe puts my worries into perspective instantly. God speaks by reminding me how tiny and how fleeting my problems really are, and by reminding me that I am not responsible for running the universe.

Whether you live in the country or in the city where you can't see the stars, when you go outdoors even for only a few minutes of retreat, there are special blessings waiting for you. It doesn't matter whether you are digging in your garden, walking the dog, sitting on a sandy beach, or just standing in a parking lot, you can enjoy a mini-retreat just by focusing all our attention on what is around you and within you.

"The world abounds with quiet, free sources of revitalization."

Melody Beattie

You may begin by noticing your immediate environment. Look around, up to the sky, and down to the ground. What do you see? Are there cars passing by? Is there a sidewalk or parking lot? Is the surface cracked or even? Or are you standing on grass? Are there people everywhere? Notice them and send each of them a blessing of peace. Be still and breathe. Feel the moment and live.

Now look more deeply. Notice the clouds or lack of clouds in the sky. Pay attention to the sunshine or the rain. See the details of your environment as if you had never been in this place before even if you are in the same place every day.
Just noticing puts you squarely in the present moment.

Now let all your senses come to life. Feel the sun shining on your face and the air against your skin. Is it dry or moist? Warm or cold? Is there a breeze blowing? Sniff the air and notice the smells. Notice any trees and plants around you. Listen to the sounds. Notice how you feel in this place and be still with those feelings for a moment.

Breathe deeply and let it be.

If you have green space around your home, if there is a park near you or on your route to work, perhaps, stop for a moment and be present there. Give your full attention to the shapes, colors and textures of the plants, flowers and grasses. Are there tiny wildflowers beneath your feet? Or lizards in the grass? Look up and see the birds. Listen to their calls. Breathe in the beauty of nature and be grateful. Then turn your attention inward and find the stillness deep within. Know that your inner space is like the green space outside – beautiful, varied, naturally ordered, growing, and bountiful. Sit for a moment with that awareness until your inner space is calm.

If you are blessed to have trees around you, notice how the breeze moves the leaves in the trees. Stand under a tree for a moment and listen to the sound that the wind makes in its branches. If there are several trees nearby, listen to each one and notice how every tree has its own unique sound. Are there other sounds you haven't

noticed before? Pay attention to them now
and be filled with wonder.

Notice that the green trees
and plants are breathing together with
you. Choose one tree, stop beside it
for a moment, and breathe with a tree.
Breathe consciously with it, exchanging
one element for another, giving life to
one another. Feel your oneness with the
tree and all living things.

Touch a leaf or a flower.
Pick up a rock, a bit of grass or soil
and hold it in your hand. Feel the
connection between yourself and the
Earth. Retreat into this oneness of life
for a moment or two. Fold your hands
together and be grateful for the Earth
that sustains your life.

When you can make time, and if you have the space, you can try creating an outdoor garden, whether for flowers or vegetables or both. After the planning is done and the seeds or small plants are purchased, the really good stuff begins – getting down on our knees and digging in the earth. As you dig, breathe deeply and smell the fresh-turned soil. Consider that all the food you eat comes from the earth; without it, there would be no life on this planet. Breathe deeply and be grateful. Look closely into a seed or plant and consider that it, like yourself, is a living being with great potential for flourishing and blooming in rich, fertile ground. Touch the tender plants or tiny seeds with reverence and tenderness as you place them in the soil. Bless each living thing with a prayer for its healthy life and growth. Water them, and as you do so, think of the living water that nourishes your soul. Be grateful for the web of life of which you are a part. Say a prayer of thanks for the rain and sunshine that help the soil bring forth good things to eat, and for all the elements that sustain your life.

If you don't have a place
to plant something outdoors, or if
your neighborhood is not safe, you
might want to create a window box
garden, or bring the outdoors in by
keeping a few plants near a sunny
window. Make the planting and
the caring for your plants a ritual
of caring for yourself and a time
of gratitude. Take a few moments
each day to be still with these living
things, touch them, smell them, and
sense your essential oneness with
them. Breathe in their
essence and be still.

You might also consider creating a sacred
space outdoors, a quiet spot where you can sit
quietly, worship or reflect. If you have the space
and the means, make a seat among the trees
and plants, or carve out a spot on the ground
and place before you a plant or other naturally

beautiful object. Add water sounds if you can – the smallest fountain or waterfall in a dish is enough – to remind you of this essential element of nature and of life. Remember that your body consists mostly of water. You come from a watery place and it is in your nature to be drawn back to that place of safety and warmth. When you have a free moment, go and sit in your special place. Listen, look, touch and feel the powerful healing force that lives within you, the essence of living water. Breathe and be grateful for your life.

No matter what you do, nature can bless you with its diversity, beauty and power. When you have more time, try spending an hour sitting in the warm sunshine or in the shade of a beloved tree. Let the wondrous beauty of nature fill your soul with peace and your heart with wonder.

Add your own ideas here:

Walking Retreat

A lthough sitting still is beneficial in many ways, when we are trying to stop our compulsive thinking and retreat from stress, it is not always necessary to be physically still in order to achieve mental stillness. Walking retreat, or walking meditation as it is sometimes called, can be especially beneficial. Whether your walk is long or short, for business or pleasure, you can make your walk a time of retreat. (You can also adapt this practice for use while running, of course.) The secret is to focus on the present moment with each step you take.

You may begin simply by counting your steps while breathing as you walk. The right count for you will be determined by your physical and emotional state, as well as your walking pace. You will need to experiment to find the most comfortable breathing count for you. In my own practice, breathing out, I usually take six steps. Breathing in, I usually take four steps. As you walk, your breathing will adjust as your body becomes warm and your walking speed increases or slows down. Everyone experiences the walking retreat in their own unique way. (Bhante Dhammawhansha)

Just a short walk down a hallway, around the living room, or from your car into a building can provide the mini-retreat you need on any given day. When walking indoors, you might be thinking like this:

Feeling my foot touch the floor, I am grateful for the solid floor beneath me. I breathe deeply as I walk. With each step I take, I observe my surroundings. I feel my feelings, and release the tension in my body.

You can use whatever time you have to continue this walking retreat until you begin to feel more relaxed.

As you walk and focus on your breathing, feel your body working. Pay attention to the muscles in your legs, the movement of your arms, the rising and falling of your chest. Smile to your heart as it beats a little faster, and be grateful for your wonderful body.

As you settle in to a comfortable pace, tune in to the quiet place within yourself. Breathe into it. See your inner self unwinding and letting go. Feel the tension in your body decreasing with each step. Straighten your shoulders and your back. Lift your chin a bit, and smile to yourself. How good it is to be alive and moving.

Try repeating a word, phrase or a simple prayer as you walk like Love, love, love, love. Peace, peace, peace, peace. Or, I am alive now. I am alive now. I am alive now. Repeat a short prayer such as, God give me peace. God give me hope. God give me strength.

Let there be joy.

Or, let there be peace. Let there be love. Let there be joy. Or, bless all living beings. Bless all living beings. Bless all living beings.

Let there be love.

You can use any words or prayer you wish, or use a simple, soothing sound like Ohm, or Ahhh, or another that resonates with you. You may make the sounds or say the words out loud, or keep them silent. Or you may sing them chant-like or with rhythm and melody. Remember that your purpose is not to sound good or to impress anyone, but to be fully present in the moment with your body, your environment, and your spirit. Whatever helps you achieve this purpose is good.

Let there be peace.

Try holding a positive vision of your good
health as you walk.
See yourself strong and feeling good.
See pain drain away. Then hold a similar
vision of persons you care about,
one at a time. See them healthy, peaceful,
and happy as you walk and breathe.
You may repeat their names in your mind
with your steps, if you like.
I say, Ri - chard, Jenn - ifer, Eli - zabeth.
Then begin to include others in your vision
- like a stranger passing by,
someone you don't know well,
then someone you do not like.
See each one of them healthy,
peaceful, and happy.
Wishing for others what we desire for
ourselves brings the same back to us.
See the circle of blessing created by your
intention and your thoughts going around
and around, spreading blessings all around.

Long walks outdoors are a real treat. It is usually best to start out slow, relaxing and breathing deeply as you go along As the walk progresses, you might walk faster or slower, depending on your needs at that moment. It is easy then to enjoy the other pleasures of an outdoor walking retreat, listening to the wind in the trees, noticing the birds, smelling the air, feeling the breeze. As you walk and breathe, you can think like this:

Feeling my foot touch the ground, I am grateful to the Earth. Breathing with the trees, I am one with the trees. Walking on the Earth, I am one with all life. Walking on the Earth, I am one with the Universe and at peace with myself and all living things.

Perhaps there is a nature path near you, or a labyrinth made just for such purposes as walking retreats. If so, you might want to try a walking retreat at one of these locations sometime soon. A half-hour walk on a beautiful path or on the beach might give you as much peace as a week-long retreat full of activities and communal meals. And when you have more time, there are usually park benches or other places for sitting and continuing in a silent retreat or meditation. Whatever you do, remember to be aware of what is happening around you and within you in this moment. This is what it means to be fully alive.

Add your ideas for more time-outs here:

Chapter Six

Going Deeper

Anytime is the right time to retreat. You have only to tune in to the precious, present moment for a wonderfully soothing, relaxing experience. During your mini-retreats, you can also tune in to your inner self to check your emotional, physical and spiritual condition. By turning your attention inward, you are taking your spiritual pulse, so to speak, and reading the internal messages that tell you so much about how you are really doing in this life. You might also find your inner connection with your Higher Power.

Many times, while taking a mini-retreat, I have found my connection to the Universe or to God is very strong I have been led into enlightening conversations with Jesus, and I have fallen directly into the arms of God. Sometimes the Presence of Spirit within looks and feels like a vibrating light, an energy field that is my life force and my purpose. This field of energy has sometimes expressed itself as a Voice of insight or wisdom, a feeling of warmth and calm, or a warm golden light. On other occasions, I experienced a shimmering, pulsating, golden egg that fills and empowers me. It is ready to open, to bless and heal me, and to shine outward to others with love and inspiration. I am always grateful for these experiences when they come, but they are relatively rare. Most often, I experience something else.

It usually takes only a few minutes to find my quiet place of retreat within, to connect with Spirit, or to check my inner condition. Fortunately, what I usually find there is good. Sometimes I am aware of a deep inner contentment, even in the face of troublesome situations. At other times, however, I find that my body is holding unexpected tension or pain, that my spirit is out of balance, or that I am more fearful, upset, or angry about something. These revelations let me know whether I need to do some work to resolve my internal issues. I might spend that time in the quiet, or reading inspirational literature and journaling, or talking with a trusted friend or professional counselor about whatever is bothering me. This process of checking in with my inner self may also reveal physical issues that require rest, a change of diet, special home care, or even professional medical attention.

Today I am not afraid to look inside myself and to feel my uncomfortable feelings because experience has taught me that what I find there always helps me grow and heal, make better decisions, take better care of myself, and respond more lovingly to others. But there was a time when I was afraid of my feelings. I avoided them at all cost for fear they would overwhelm me. This was not a conscious fear, but it was very real, nonetheless, and it kept me from experiencing personal growth for many years. The only way I was able to overcome that fear was to face the feelings, walk through them, and come out on the other side. With loving friends to provide guidance, support and encouragement, I found out that feeling my feelings, no matter how painful they were, would not kill me. Not feeling them, however, probably would have.

"You, the richest person on Earth, who have been going around begging for a living, stop being the destitute child. Come back and claim your heritage."

Thich Nhat Hanh.

What you will find when you turn your attention inward will be unique to you. It will be a reflection of your personal, spiritual and emotional condition, as well as your physical well-being. Whatever trouble spots you might discover during your inner journey are important messengers that should be honored and respected. If you ignore or deny them, they will likely grow more intense and troublesome.

Resolving long-standing inner issues usually requires more than daily mini-retreats. It takes what it takes. Sometimes a professional counselor or spiritual mentor is needed; sometimes not. With the proper care and attention over time, however, emotionally and spiritually painful places can be healed and serenity may return.

All the practices described in this book can also be extended and expanded to include an inner walk through the painful, or secret places that develop in each of us in the course of human life – if that is what you want to do. By walking through those places of woundedness, you will have the opportunity to release your pain. If you are not ready to dig deeper just now, do not judge or criticize yourself. I trust that your Higher Power will lead you through a deeper journey inward when and if the time is right for you.

While time is limited, you can practice mini-retreats to find the peace and comfort you need to get through the few minutes, the next hour, or the remainder of the day. When you are ready, you may come back to the mini-retreat practices you have already developed, study more contemplative and meditative techniques if you wish, ask for help when needed, and sit (or walk) with your deeper feelings for longer periods. You will probably find that when you allow your feelings to be and honor them in the stillness without acting on them right away, the feelings will begin to diminish or soften. By taking care of your feelings, you are taking care of your deeper self. By going to your peaceful, quiet place within, you can connect with your

Inner Wisdom, the Divine Presence, and gain perspective on and insight into the problems that affect your life. Treat your feelings as wisely, gently, patiently and lovingly as you would a little child, and in time, they will grow up, and you will experience more peace.

In the meantime, or if all is well in your life, I invite you to join me in making mini-retreats part of your everyday practice of living well. I am sure that these brief time-outs will enrich your life-experiences, improve your sense of well-being, and deepen your connection with Spirit.

May you always be richly blessed with love, good health, a sense of purpose, and peace.

Other resources from Mary Dawn Pyle include a guided meditation CD, "Journey into Presence", spiritual development and recovery classes, workshops, and personal spiritual mentoring

Visit www.marydawnpyle.com for more information on how to access these resources.

This book is intended as a supplement to, not a substitute for, medical, spiritual, psychological or other support that might be needed.

Mary Dawn Pyle, M.A.,

is an author, speaker, teacher and spiritual mentor.

Mary Dawn is a former Hospice Chaplain. She holds a Masters in Religious Studies and has experience as a retreat leader, director of adult church ministries, and a counselor in alcohol and drug treatment programs. She is also an experienced Reiki Master.

Mary Dawn has recently released a guided meditation CD called "Journey into Presence," which is available online from CDBaby, DigStation, Amazon.com, iTunes, and other sites.

She is also a professor at St. Petersburg College in Pinellas County, Florida, where she has taught World Religions and Applied Ethics.

She is a co-author and co-editor of Ethics Applied, Edition 5.0, and Business Ethics Applied, along with numerous magazine and newspaper articles. She has also won an award for poetry from the Florida Writers Association.

Mary Dawn lives with her husband and one happy, playful dog near the Florida Gulf Coast.

You can find her at:

www.marydawnpyle.com.

CPSIA information can be obtained at www.ICGtesting.com
Printed in the USA
LVOW010340171011

250759LV00001B/1/P